DIVINE MANIFESTATIONS

(Tajallīyāt-e-Ilāhiyyah)

Ḥaḍrat Mirza Ghulam Ahmad of Qadian
THE PROMISED MESSIAH AND MAHDI,
FOUNDER OF THE AHMADIYYA MUSLIM JAMĀ'AT

ISLAM INTERNATIONAL PUBLICATIONS LIMITED

تجلیات الهیه

(*Tajallīyāt-e-Ilāhiyyah*)
Divine Manifestations

First Edition (Urdu): 1922, Qadian
First English Edition: 2006, London

© Islam International Publications Ltd.

Published by:
Islam International Publications Ltd.
'Islamabad' Sheephatch Lane,
Tilford, Surrey GU10 2AQ
United Kingdom.

Printed in U. K. at:
Raqeem Press
Tilford, Surrey

ISBN: 1 85372 948 5

ABOUT THE AUTHOR

Born in 1835 in Qadian (India), Ḥaḍrat Mirza Ghulam Ahmad, the Promised Messiah and Mahdi[as], remained dedicated to the study of the Holy Quran and to a life of prayer and devotion. Finding Islam the target of foul attacks from all directions, the fortunes of Muslims at a low ebb, faith yielding to doubt and religion only skin-deep, he undertook vindication and exposition of Islam. In his vast corpus of writings (including his epoch-making *'Brāhīn-e-Aḥmadiyyah'*), his lectures, discourses, religious debates etc., he argued that Islam was a living faith and the only faith by following which man could establish contact with his Creator and enter into communion with Him. The teachings contained in the Holy Quran and the Law promulgated by Islam were designed to raise man to moral, intellectual and spiritual perfection. He announced that God had appointed him the Messiah and Mahdi as mentioned in the prophecies of the Bible, the Holy Quran and *Aḥādīth*. In 1889 he began to accept initiation into his Community which is now established in one hundred and seventy-six countries. His eighty books are written mostly in Urdu, but some are in Arabic and Persian.

After his demise in 1908, the Promised Messiah[as] was succeeded by Ḥaḍrat Maulawī Nūr-ud-Dīn[ra], Khalīfatul Masīḥ I. On the death of Ḥaḍrat Maulawī Nūr-ud-Dīn[ra] in 1914, Ḥaḍrat Mirza Bashīr-ud-Dīn Mahmood Ahmad[ra], who was also the Promised Messiah's[as] Promised Son, was elected as Khalifa. Ḥaḍrat Mirza Bashīr-ud-Dīn Mahmood Ahmad[ra] remained in office for nearly fifty two years. He died in 1965 and was succeeded by his eldest son, Ḥaḍrat Hafiz Mirza Nasir Ahmad[rh], the Promised grandson of the Promised Messiah[as]. After seventeen years of meritorious services he passed away in 1982. He was succeeded by his younger brother, Ḥaḍrat Mirza Tahir Ahmad[rh] as Khalīfatul Masīḥ IV who, having led the Community to its present strength and global recognition, passed away on the 19th April 2003. Ḥaḍrat Mirza Masroor Ahmad Khalīfatul Masīḥ V[at] is the present head of the Community and enjoys the distinction of being the great-grandson of Ḥaḍrat Mirza Ghulam Ahmad[as].

CONTENTS

1. Foreword vii
2. Publisher's Note ix
3. Text 1-36
4. An Important Note 37

Foreword

Tajallīyāt-e-Ilāhiyyah is an unfinished book of the Promised Messiah[as], written in 1906 and published posthumously in 1922.

The book covers important subjects of Divine knowledge and spiritual insight. It opens with an account of the precision with which the Promised Messiah's prophecies regarding earthquakes had been fulfilled, and foretells the coming of five more terrible catastrophes. In this context, Ḥuḍūr[as] also explains the philosophy behind Divine chastisement.

The difference between Divine and Satanic dreams, an account of the fulfilment of the prophecy regarding 'Abdullāh Ātham, and a profound prophecy about global acceptance and victory of Ahmadiyyat—the true Islam—are but a few of the many singular themes discussed in this book.

The original English translation, which was done by Mr. Mubarak Ahmad Nazir (Canada), has gone through several revisions. For these we are indebted to Mr. Malik Mahmood Ahmad (Islamabad), Mr. Munawwar Ahmad Saeed (USA) and Ms. Uzma Aftab (Lahore). I am also very grateful to Mr. Ata-ul-Mannan Raja and Mr. Tahir Mahmood Mubashar of Wakālat Taṣnīf, who very ably assisted me in the whole project. Last but not least, we are grateful to Maulana Munir-ud-Din Shams, Additional Wakīlut Taṣnīf, London, for his kind help and suggestions. Mirza Anas Ahmad M.A., M.Litt. (OXON) Wakīlul Ishā'at, Tahrik-e-Jadid, pointed out to me mistakes in the final revised draft of the English translation, so the final revision was done by me. He also found the references of *Aḥādīth* mentioned in the book. I am very grateful to him, and his team, especially Shaikh Naseer Ahmad who did most of the work of formatting and desktop publishing and Shahid Mahmood Ahmad, Sayyed Mansoor Ahmad Bashir who did the final proof reading of the manuscript. May Allah reward them all.

Muhammad 'Alī Chaudhry
Wakīlut Taṣnīf,
Rabwah.
Sunday, 18 June 2006

Publisher's Note

We feel honoured to publish Divine Manifestations, the English translation of *Tajallīyāt-e-Ilāhiyyah* written in Urdu in 1906 by the Promised Messiah[as], Ḥaḍrat Mirza Ghulam Ahmad and posthumously published in 1922. This is the first edition of English translation. The following features of this edition should be kept in mind.

This is the translation from the first Urdu edition of the book.

The way the Promised Messiah[as] has paragraphed the book is not followed: paragraphs are given according to the modern standard practice.

The references of *Aḥādīth* quoted by the Promised Messiah[as] are supplied as footnotes. They are marked with asterisk *. On page 9, the Promised Messiah[as] has made a reference to the Holy Quran without giving the verse: we have given the chapter and verse reference in the footnote marked with asterisk *.

The words in the text in normal brackets ( ) and in between the long dashes — are the words of the Promised Messiah[as] and if any explanatory words or phrases are added by the translator for the purpose of clarification, they are put in square brackets [ ].

The name of Muhammad[sa], the Holy Prophet of Islam, has been followed by the symbol [sa], which is an abbreviation for the salutation *Ṣallallāhu 'Alaihi*

Wasallam (may peace and blessings of Allah be upon him). The names of other Prophets and Messengers are followed by the symbol ^{as}, an abbreviation for *'Alaihissalām* (on whom be peace). The actual salutations have not generally been set out in full, but they should nevertheless, be understood as being repeated in full in each case. The symbol ^{ra} is used with the name of the Companions of the Holy Prophet^{sa} and those of the Promised Messiah^{as}. It stands for *Raḍī Allāhu 'anhu/'anhā/'anhum* (May Allah be pleased with him/with her/with them). ^{rh} stands for *Raḥimahullāhu Ta'ālā* (may Allah have mercy on him). ^{at} stands for *Ayyadahullāhu Ta'ālā* (May Allah, the Mighty help him).

In transliterating Arabic words we have followed the following system adopted by the Royal Asiatic Society.

ا at the beginning of a word, pronounced as *a*, *i*, *u* preceded by a very slight aspiration, like *h* in the English word 'honour'.

ث *th*, pronounced like th in the English word 'thing'.

ح *ḥ*, a guttural aspirate, stronger than h.

خ *kh*, pronounced like the Scotch ch in 'loch'.

ذ *dh*, pronounced like the English th in 'that'.

ص *ṣ*, strongly articulated s.

ض *ḍ*, similar to the English th in 'this'.

ط	*t*, strongly articulated palatal t.
ظ	*z̧*, strongly articulated z.
ع	', a strong guttural, the pronunciation of which must be learnt by the ear.
غ	*gh*, a sound approached very nearly in the r *'grasseye'* in French, and in the German r. It requires the muscles of the throat to be in the 'gargling' position whilst pronouncing it.
ق	*q*, a deep guttural k sound.
ء	', a sort of catch in the voice.

Short vowels are represented by:

a for ―◌َ― (like *u* in 'bud');

i for ―◌ِ― (like *i* in 'bid');

u for ―◌ُ― (like *oo* in 'wood');

Long vowels by:

ā for ―◌ا― or آ (like *a* in 'father');

ī for ی ―◌ِ― or ―◌ِی― (like *ee* in 'deep');

ū for و ―◌ُ― (like *oo* in 'root');

Other:

ai for ی ―◌َ― (like *i* in 'site')◆;

au for و ―◌َ― (resembling *ou* in 'sound').

The consonants not included in the above list have the

◆ In Arabic words like شیخ (Shaikh) there is an element of diphthong which is missing when the word is pronounced in Urdu.

same phonetic value as in the principal languages of Europe.

We have not transliterated Arabic, Persian and Urdu words which have become part of English language, e.g., Islam, Mahdi, Quran, Hijra, Ramadan, Rahman, Hadith, Zakat, ulema, umma, sunna, kafir etc.

For quotes straight commas (straight quotes) are used to differentiate them from the curved commas used in the system of transliteration, ' for ع, ' for ء. Commas as punctuation marks are used according to the normal usage.

References of the Holy Quran are given as Chapter No. followed by colon followed by Verse No. Thus 2:43 means Chapter 2 and Verse 43 of the Holy Quran. The same rule is followed in giving references of the Bible.

Publishers

$$\text{بِسْمِ اللّٰهِ الرَّحْمٰنِ الرَّحِيْمِ}^1$$

$$\text{نَحْمَدُهٗ وَ نُصَلِّىْ عَلٰى رَسُوْلِهِ الْكَرِيْمِ}^2$$

"A Warner came unto the world, but the world accepted him not, but God will accept him and establish his truth by mighty assaults."

The Prophecy of the Almighty God Regarding the Coming of Five Earthquakes
The Words of Which are

"Five times shall I show you the dazzling manifestation of this Sign."

The meaning of this Divine revelation is that God Almighty says that, in order to bear witness to the truth of my claim, and so that people may realize that I am from Him, God Almighty will cause five terrifying earthquakes to appear, one following the other, at short intervals. They will bear witness to the truth of my claim, and each of them will display such radiance that the beholder will at once be reminded of God. Such a terrifying effect will they have on

---

[1] In the name of Allah, the Gracious, the Merciful. [Publisher]
[2] We praise Allah and invoke blessings upon His noble Prophet[sa]. [Publisher]

people's hearts, and so extraordinary will be their power, intensity and devastation, that people beholding them will lose their very senses. All this will be the result of Divine jealousy, for people did not recognize the Hour. God says, I was hidden but now I shall make Myself known, and I shall display My Brilliance and liberate My servants, just as Moses and his people were liberated from the hands of Pharaoh. These miracles shall be manifested in the same way as those displayed by Moses in the presence of Pharaoh. And God says that He shall make a clear distinction between the truthful and the liar, and He shall support the one who is from Him and oppose anyone who opposes His chosen one.[3]

So O ye who hear, if these prophecies come to be fulfilled in just an ordinary way, then know that I am not from God, but if these prophecies do create a panic in the world at the time of their fulfilment, and their severity leads people to the verge of insanity, and there is widespread loss of life and property, then fear God Who made all this happen for my sake. How

---

[3] While [I was] in a state of slight drowsiness, God showed me a paper on which was written:

$$تِلْكَ اٰیَاتُ الْکِتَابِ الْمُبِیْنِ$$

which means that they [the earthquakes] will be the signs of the truth of the Holy Quran. [Author] can man run away from God Who has control over every speck and particle? He says that He will close in stealthily, like thieves do, meaning thereby that no astrologer, seer or dreamer will have any knowledge of the exact time of the occurrence of these happenings, except to the extent to which He has conveyed it to His Promised Messiah or may later augment thereon.

There will be a change in the world after these signs and many hearts shall be drawn towards God. In many blessed hearts the love of the world shall grow cold, and veils of indifference shall be lifted, and they shall be made to drink the elixir of True Islam. As God Himself has said:

چو دَورِ خسروی آغاز کردند

مسلماں را مسلماں باز کردند [4]

'Khosrau's era' refers to the era of the Call of this humble one. But it does not suggest earthly kingdom, rather it signifies the heavenly kingdom which I have been given. What this revelation briefly means is that in the era of Khosrau, i.e., the era of the Messiah—which in God's sight is called a Heavenly kingdom—

---

[4] At the beginning of Khosrau's era, Muslims, who are Muslims in name only, will become true Muslims. [Translator]

began at the end of the sixth millennium, as prophesised by God's holy Messengers[as]. The result was that those who were Muslims only in name started becoming true Muslims, as nearly four hundred thousand have already done. I am much gratified that at my hand almost four hundred thousand have repented of their sins and they include many Hindus as well as English people. Only yesterday, in fact, a Hindu was initiated as a Muslim at my hand and was given the name Muhammad Iqbal. Yesterday, when I was repeatedly reciting the above Divine Revelation, my spirit was all of a sudden imbibed with the following words which are a sequel to the above revelation:

مــقـــام او مبیــں از راہ تــحقیــر

بــدورانـــش رســولاں ناز کردند [5]

Likewise, in the following revelation, I was given the glad tidings of the spread of Islam through me. God addressed me saying:

يَا قَمَرُ يَا شَمْسُ اَنْتَ مِنِّى وَ اَنَا مِنْكَ

that is, 'O Moon and O Sun! You are of Me and I am of you.' In this Divine Revelation, God has first called

---

[5] Do not look down with disdain at his stature,
For even the Prophets take pride in his era. [Translator]

me the moon and given Himself the title of the Sun. This means that just as the moon receives its glow through the bounty and benevolence of the sun, so is my light a result of the bounty and beneficence of God. Then God has called Himself the Moon and named me the sun. This indicates that He will manifest His glorious light through me. He was hidden, but shall now be manifested through me. The world was unaware of His radiance, but now, through me, His awe-inspiring light will spread all over the world. Just as a bolt of lightning illuminates the whole sky in a flash, so shall all this come to pass in this age.

God addresses me and says, 'For your sake I descended upon the earth, and for you did My name shine, and I have selected you out of the whole world.' And He says:

قَالَ رَبُّكَ اِنَّهُ نَازِلٌ مِّنَ السَّمَآءِ مَا يُرْضِيْكَ

that is, 'Your God says that such powerful miracles will descend from the heavens that you shall be pleased.' Out of these, an epidemic of the plague and two powerful earthquakes—of which I had foretold in accordance with Divine revelation—have already appeared in this country. But now, God says that five more earthquakes are to appear. The world shall see their extraordinary radiance and shall know as a certainty that they are the signs which have appeared in support of His servant, the Promised Messiah. It is unfortunate indeed that the astrologers and fortune-tellers of this age contend with me in matters of prophecies just as the magicians had confronted Prophet Moses[as]. Some ignorant claimants to revelation, who lie in pits of darkness, contest with me like Bal'am, abandoning the truth and abetting the misguided. But God says that He will put all of them to shame and shall never grant this distinction to anyone else. Now is the time for them all to confront me with their horoscopes or their revelations. And if they now spare me any of their onslaughts, they shall surely be the losers. God says: 'I shall defeat them all and shall become the enemy of thy enemies.' He says, 'I have chosen thee for the manifestation of My mysteries, and the earth and the heavens are with you just as they are with Me. You are to Me as is My throne.' In support of [this revelation], there is the following verse in the Holy Quran which distinguishes God's chosen Prophets[as] from others:

لَا يُظْهِرُ عَلٰى غَيْبِهٖ اَحَداً اِلَّا مَنِ ارْتَضٰى مِنْ رَّسُوْلٍ [6]

---

[6] Al-Jinn, 72:27-28. [Publisher]

That is, crystal clear knowledge of the unseen is only revealed to His chosen Messenger. No one else has any share in it.

Hence, members of our Community should not stumble, nor should they give any credence to my opponents and to those who have not been initiated at my hand, or else they will come under Divine wrath. Whenever some foul-mouthed person makes a false prophecy, God puts to test the truly faithful ones to see whether they give such a person the respect and regard which should be given only to God and to His Messenger. He watches whether or not they are firmly established upon the truth which they have been given.

Remember, when these five earthquakes will have passed, and the destruction which God has willed shall have taken place, His mercy shall once again surge forth and, for a time, extraordinary and fearful earthquakes shall cease. The epidemic of the plague too shall disappear from the land, just as God addressed me and said:

يَأْتِيْ عَلٰى جَهَنَّمَ زَمَانٌ لَّيْسَ فِيْهَآ اَحَدٌ

That is, a time will eventually come upon this Hell—the hell of plagues and earthquakes—when none shall be left in it, meaning, [none shall remain in hell] in this country. And just as it happened at the time of Noah[as] that a period of calm was granted after many people had been killed, the same shall happen now. Following this revelation, God says:

$$ثُمَّ يُغَاثُ النَّاسُ وَ هُمْ يَعْصِرُوْنَ$$

That is, that people's supplications will then be heard, rains shall come on time and the orchards and fields shall bear fruit in abundance. A period of joy shall begin and extraordinary calamities shall recede, lest people should think that God is only the Avenger (*Qahhār*) and not Merciful (*Raḥīm*) and consider His Messiah to be ill-omened.[7]

Remember, it was necessary for large number of people to die at the time of the Messiah and it was also destined that plagues and earthquakes should strike. This is the meaning of the Hadith wherein it is written that people would perish with the breath of the

---

[7] It has been destined from the very beginning that the Promised Messiah would first appear in an awe-striking form, and, as far as his eyes would see, people would perish with his breath. This means that that will not be the time for Jihad or fighting with the sword. It will be the spiritual attention of the Messiah which will work like a sword, and awe-inspiring signs like plagues, earthquakes and other calamities shall descend from heaven. Then God's Messiah shall look upon mankind with compassion, and the heavens too shall show signs of compassion, and people shall be blessed with long lives and abundant provisions shall come out of the earth. [Author]

Messiah, and his killing breath would work as far as his eyes would see*. It is wrong to infer from this Hadith that the Messiah would be a witch that would remove people's hearts just by looking at them. What it really means is that wherever his pure breath—i.e. his teachings—would spread in the world, people would deny him, reject him and abuse him; so much so, that their rejection shall become a cause of chastisement for them.⁸ This Hadith indicates that the Promised Messiah will be vehemently opposed, with the result that a great many people shall die in the

---

* See *Ṣaḥīḥ Muslim, Kitābul Fitan, Bābu Dhikril Dajjāl.* [Publisher]

⁸ This Hadith, too, proves that, at the time of the Messiah, the injunction regarding Jihad shall be suspended, in accordance with one of the characteristics of the Promised Messiah recorded in *Ṣaḥīḥ Bukhārī* is يضع الحرب* i.e., when the Promised Messiah comes, he shall put an end to war and Jihad. The underlying wisdom of this saying is that since the mere spiritual attention of the Messiah will be sufficient to trigger wrathful signs and hundreds of thousands shall die in plagues and earthquakes, it will not be necessary to destroy anyone with the sword. And God is far too Compassionate to inflict two terrible signs upon a people at the same time, i.e., the vengeance of God coupled with the destruction unleashed by people through the sword. God Almighty has clearly stated in the Holy Quran that these two punishments cannot come together at the same time.** [Author]

* *Ṣaḥīḥ Bukhārī, Kitābul Ḥadīthul Ambiyā', Bāb Nazūlul Masīḥ.* In some editions of *Bukhārī* the words are يضع الجزية ; however, both the expressions virtually mean the same thing—for *Jizya* (a kind of tax) is taken from the vanquished non-Muslims. [Publisher]

** See the Holy Quran, Al-An'ām 6:66. [Publisher]

land, the most severe earthquakes shall take place and peace shall disappear altogether. It would otherwise be irrational to think that pious and righteous people should be subjected to various punishments without any reason. This is the reason why, even in the past, ignorant people have considered Prophets[as] to be bearers of misfortune and have blamed them for what were actually the consequences of their own misdeeds. The fact, however, is that it is not the Prophet who brings punishment; rather it is the fact that people have become deserving of punishment that brings a Prophet as a final warning and produces the necessity for his advent. Severe punishment never takes place without the advent of a Prophet, as God says in the Holy Quran:

وَ مَا كُنَّا مُعَذِّبِيْنَ حَتّٰى نَبْعَثَ رَسُوْلاً [9]

Why then is it that the epidemic of the plague is devouring the country on the one hand, and terrifying earthquakes are giving no respite on the other? O heedless ones, look around! May be a Prophet has been established by God and it is him you have rejected.[10] It is already the twenty-fourth year of the

---

[9] 'We do not punish a people until a Prophet has been sent to them.'- (Banī Isrā'īl, 17:16) **[Publisher]**
[10] In the context of the present age, God only uses the world *Nabī* [Prophet] for a person who has been honoured with converse with

Hijri century. Why, without the advent of a Prophet, are you being afflicted with this calamity which takes away your friends and loved ones each year and brings sorrow to your hearts? There must be a reason, why do you not look for it? And why do you not reflect upon the verse which I have quoted above, in which God Almighty says:

$$\text{وَ مَا كُنَّا مُعَذِّبِيْنَ حَتّٰى نَبْعَثَ رَسُوْلاً}^{11}$$

That is, We never send an extraordinary punishment upon a people until We have sent a Messenger to fully convey Our message.

Just consider this: Is it not an extraordinary calamity with which you have been afflicted for some years now? The afflictions which you witness today are such as your forefathers could never have imagined and are beyond anything this land has seen for thousands of years. The plague and the earthquake which you see today, I have been seeing them in the

---

Him and is entrusted with the revival of religion. Not that such a person will introduce any new Shariah, because the Shariah culminated with the Holy Prophet[sa], and, after the Holy Prophet[sa], the word *Nabī* cannot be used for any person unless he is also called *Ummatī* [the follower of the Holy Prophet[sa]], which means that everything he has been blessed with is through his obedience to the Holy Prophet[sa] and not directly. [Author]

[11] The Holy Quran, Banī Isrā'īl 17:16 [Publisher]

realm of *Kashf*[12] for the past twenty-five years. If God did not give me news of these calamities beforehand, then I am false. But if these predictions have been recorded in my books for the last twenty-five years, and I have continually warned you about them,[13] then you should beware of coming under Divine censure.

You have already heard that, one year before it happened, I had published in the newspapers the prophecy regarding the earthquake which took place on 4 April 1905. That prophecy contained not only the words:

"زلزلہ کا دھکّا"[14]

but also the Revelation:

عَفَتِ الدِّيَارُ مَحَلُّهَا وَ مُقَامُهَا

Which means that in some parts of the Punjab buildings would collapse and disappear. I need not dwell on how very clearly this prophecy came to be fulfilled.

Then, in the same month of April, I published

---

[12] *Kashf*, (plural *Kushūf*): Divinely inspired visions which are experienced in a state of wakefulness. [Translator]
[13] The prophecies regarding these appalling earthquakes were published in my book *Brāhīn-e-Ahmadiyyah* twenty-five years ago. [Author]
[14] 'Jolt of earthquake.' [Translator]

another prophecy which God had revealed to me, that just as the earthquake of 4th April 1905 struck in spring, the other earthquake would also strike in spring and not before. That earthquake, therefore, cannot strike earlier than 25 February 1906.[15]

Hence, no earthquake took place in the next eleven months. But when the date of 25 February 1906 had passed, such a severe earthquake struck at 1:00 a. m. on the night of 27th February 1906—right in Spring—that even the English newspapers like *The Civil and Military Gazette* conceded that it was equal in intensity to the earthquake of 4 April 1905. There was great loss of life and property in Rampur city, Simla and in many other places. It was the same earthquake about which, eleven months ago, I had been granted knowledge through this Divine Revelation:

[16] "پھر بہار آئی خدا کی بات پھر پوری ہوئی"

The earthquake, accordingly, struck in spring. Reflect upon this! Is there anyone besides God who can make these predictions with such precision? I did not possess any power over the earth's layers that I could

---

[15] The date when spring formally begins in India. [Publisher]
[16] 'Spring comes again, and the Word of God is once again fulfilled.' [Translator]

hold them for eleven months and then give them a powerful jolt just after 25 February 1906.

So my dear ones, now that you have witnessed these two earthquakes, it should be easy for you to understand that my prediction about the next five earthquakes is also no idle talk. You can also appreciate that just as it seemed impossible for people to believe that no earthquake, equalling the magnitude of the April earthquake, would strike the land for the succeeding eleven months, and one earthquake would strike exactly in spring, after 25th February 1906; in the same way, it now seems beyond the power of man to believe that five powerful earthquakes are to follow, through which God shall display the dazzling glow of His countenance in such a way that those who do not believe in His existence will be forced to confess that He does indeed exist. After that, there will be peace and the world will return to normality. Then, for a long time, there will be no such earthquakes.

You can well understand that no authority in the science of seismology could make such clear and precise predictions. But God, Who is Master of the heavens and earth, reveals the unknown to none but His chosen Messengers, so that people may be saved from denial and disbelief, and so that they may believe and be saved from the torment of hell. I present the heaven and earth as my witness that this day I have clearly informed you of the prophecy regarding the five earthquakes. This should serve as proof that you were properly warned, and so that death should not strike you while you are astray.

O dear ones, do not fight God, for you can never win this battle. God does not, and never has, sent down such severe punishment upon a people without first sending His Messenger to them, that is to say, until a Messenger who has been sent by Him has appeared among them. Hence, make use of this age-old law of God. Look for the person for whom, right before your eyes, the sun and moon were eclipsed in the month of Ramadan, the plague spread upon the earth and earthquakes struck. Who was it that conveyed the prophecies to you before their time, and who was it that claimed, 'I am the Promised Messiah.' Find that person, for he is present among you, and he is none other than the one who now speaks to you.

[17] وَلَا تَايْئَسُوْا مِنْ رَّوْحِ اللّٰهِ ۖ اِنَّهٗ لَا يَايْئَسُ مِنْ رَّوْحِ اللّٰهِ اِلَّا الْقَوْمُ الْكٰفِرُوْنَ

---

[17] And despair not of the mercy of Allāh; for none despair of Allāh's mercy save the unbelieving people. (The Holy Quran, Yūsuf 12:88) **[Publisher]**

At this point, I had concluded the subject, but today, Thursday 15 March 1906, I received the following revelation at dawn:

خدا نکلنے کو ہے[18]

اَنْتَ مِنِّی بِمَنْزِلَةِ بُرُوْزِیْ۔ وَعْدَ اللّٰهِ اِنَّ وَعْدَ اللّٰهِ لَا يُبَدَّلُ

meaning that God will reveal His face through these five earthquakes and will manifest His Self, and [God revealed that]: 'You are to Me like My Own Manifestation', i.e., your coming will be just like My Own Coming. This is God's promise which He will manifest Himself through five earthquakes. And God's promise will not be deferred and must come to pass.

It should be remembered that prophecies are of two kinds. First, there are simple warnings, the sole purpose of which is to punish and chastise. If such a warning comes from God Almighty, it can be averted through expressions of fear and repentance, and seeking forgiveness, or giving of alms and offering supplications. The prophecy made by the Prophet Jonah[as], for instance, was averted and did not come to pass. Prophet Jonah[as] had been told, as a warning, that punishment would come down upon his people within

---

[18] God is about to reveal Himself. [Translator]

forty days. Although this prophecy was absolute and unconditional, yet when the people of Jonah^{as} were gripped with fear, and begged forgiveness from God, and repented of their sins, the categorical promise was withheld. This put Jonah^{as} in a great predicament. He did not want to show his face to his people, after having been branded a liar.

The fact that Divine warnings can be averted through repentance, seeking forgiveness and giving of alms is something which no religion or sect denies. All Prophets are unanimous in their belief that genuine remorse, prayers and charity can ward off calamities. It is, therefore, quite obvious that when God intends to chastise someone and informs a Prophet beforehand of the impending punishment, this is then called a prophecy of warning. When a Prophet is not informed beforehand of an impending punishment, then that chastisement will be considered a hidden decree of God.

Look, how the ignorance of the foolish *Maulawīs* is exposed when they object that Deputy 'Abdullāh Ātham did not die within the period of fifteen months, but that he died a few months later. They are ignorant of the fact that this was a prophecy which contained a warning. It was not unconditional, as was the prophecy of Jonah[as], and was accompanied by the words: 'Provided that he did not seriously incline towards the truth', which means that he would die within fifteen months, provided that his heart did not turn towards the truth. But it has been testified even by the Christians that at the very meeting where this prophecy was announced, 'Abdullāh Ātham had inclined towards the truth and was seized with fear. At the end of the debate, when I addressed Mr. 'Abdullāh Ātham aloud at the house of Dr. Martyn Clarke, in the presence of sixty or seventy witnesses, amongst whom were both Muslims and Christians, I said: 'In one of your books, you have referred to our Prophet Muhammad[sa] as the Antichrist, and, as a consequence, God had ordained that you shall perish within fifteen months, provided you do not turn towards the truth.' As soon as he heard this announcement, he was seized with fear and his face turned pale. He stuck out his tongue, held his ears with his hands[19] and, shaking with fear and with a remorseful expression on his face, said: 'I have never referred to the Holy Prophet[sa] as the Antichrist.'

I believe that more than thirty Christians, including Dr. Martyn Clarke—who is still alive—

---

[19] A traditional gesture of repentance. [Translator]

were present at the meeting. I am sure that, if asked upon oath, they will not conceal the truth or give false testimony. Furthermore, it is an established fact that, after hearing this prophecy, Deputy 'Abdullāh Ātham became extremely nervous and agitated, as if he were insane, and would often weep. From that moment on, he never published even a single line against Islam until he was overtaken by death a few months later.

During this time, I continued to publish posters challenging him to swear under oath that he had not repented as was stipulated in the text of my revelation. If he swore to this, I promised to award him a sum of four thousand rupees without delay. But, despite the plea by many Christians (encouraging him to take the oath), he never took the oath, making the excuse that it is unlawful to swear under oath in his religion, although it is evident from the Bible that St Peter, St Paul and even Jesus Christ himself swore under oath. How then could it be forbidden? To this day, all Christian witnesses swear on oath in courts. While non-Christian witnesses make a solemn declaration to speak the truth, Christians are asked to swear under oath. Anyhow, despite his evasiveness and excuses, he could not avert his doom. Just as I had publicised through posters, he died a few months after the publication of my final announcement about him. In fact, the illness that caused his death had began during those very days.

This is the standard of objections which are raised against us by the *Maulawīs*, who have derived no benefit from their study of the Quran and Hadith. Even now they cannot understand the difference between a prophecy which contains warning and one which contains an unconditional promise. They are still ignorant of the story of Jonah[as] which appears in detail even in *Durr-e-Manthūr*[*].

Since their intentions are dishonest, when they raise their objections they forget that more than ten thousand prophecies have all been fulfilled exactly as God had communicated to me. And if there happens to be a prophecy of warning, which is intended to forewarn an individual about punishment, and is held in abeyance, they raise an outcry. This proves that they have no faith in the revealed books of God. In their eagerness to attack me, they attack all the Prophets[as]. These ignorant people do not realize that, though Deputy 'Abdullāh Ātham did not die within fifteen months, he did ultimately die a few months later during my lifetime. The words of the prophecy clearly stated that the liar would die during the

---

[*] A book of exegesis of the Holy Quran by Suyūṭī. **[Publisher]**

lifetime of the truthful. He held Christianity to be true, while I claimed that Islam is the true religion. So God caused him to perish within my lifetime and established my truthfulness.

Is this the standard of the *Maulawīs'* honesty that they keep harping upon 'the fifteen months', and do not mention the other aspects of the prophecy? They do not realize that in the case of Jonah^{as} there was a categorical prophecy that chastisement would fall upon his people within forty days, but that chastisement never came and Jonah^{as} died during the lifetime of many of his people.

Alas! if these people had any honest intentions, they would—after the incident of 'Abdullāh Ātham—have at least reflected upon the clear fulfilment of the prophecy regarding Lekh Ram, which not only foretold the exact time and mode of death, but did not have any conditions attached to it either. But how can we expect those, whose hearts have become darkened by prejudice, to ponder over these matters? If they had an iota of fairness in their hearts, they could have undertaken an easy test by providing me with a written list of all my prophecies which they think have not been fulfilled, to see how many [of those] there are. Then they would obtain proof from me of those that were fulfilled, and how many those are. By this simple method, all doubts would have been lifted from their hearts. I swear by God that the prophecies giving them any cause for objection number no more than one or two, and these are prophecies of warning which were conditional and were held in abeyance in view of the dread and fear they caused, and, in accordance with the age-old custom of God that repentance, alms-giving and supplication avert such calamities. In contrast, there are over ten thousand prophecies that were fulfilled and are witnessed by hundreds of thousands of people from all sects and denominations including Muslims, Hindus and Christians who cannot help but to testify to the literal fulfilment of those prophecies. Is it being honest to disregard, and derive no benefit from a host of fulfilled prophecies for which there are a multitude of witnesses, and continue to harp upon the deferring of one or two conditional prophecies, when the deferment was in accordance with the age-old Divine practice? With this approach, the Prophethood of none of the Prophets can be established, because such instances can be found in every Prophethood. This is why I say that these people are enemies of religion and truth. Even now if a group of them are willing to cleanse their hearts and to come to me, I am ready to respond to their doubts and flimsy objections and to show them the vast number of prophecies that God has fulfilled in such a way that their truth is as bright as the rising of the sun.

If these ignorant *Maulawīs* choose to deliberately close their eyes, it is up to them. They can do no harm to the truth. But the time comes when many Pharaoh-natured people will ponder over these prophecies and be saved from drowning. God says: 'I shall mount attack after attack, until I have established your truth in the depths of their hearts.'

So, O *Maulawīs*! if you possess the strength to battle with God, then carry on. Was the humble Son of Mary, before me, spared any torment at the hands of the Jews? They even thought that they had crucified him, but God saved him from death upon the cross. So, while there was a time when he was considered no more than a fraud and a liar, another era dawned when his greatness was accepted in the hearts of people. Now there are four hundred million people who worship him as God. Although, they committed an act of disbelief by making God of a humble man, it serves as a befitting reply to the Jews that the same Jesus, Son of Mary, whom they regarded as a liar and wished to trample under their feet, has now reached such glory that four hundred million people prostrate themselves before him, and kings bow their heads in respect at the very mention of his name.

Although I have prayed that I should not become an instrument for the promotion of idolatry, as happened with Jesus, Son of Mary—and I am sure God will not let this happen—God has informed me again and again that He will grant me great glory and will instil my love in people's hearts. He shall spread my Movement all over the world and shall make my sect triumphant over all other sects. The members of my sect shall so excel in knowledge and insight that they will confound everyone with the light of their truth, and by dint of their arguments and signs. Every nation will drink of this fountain, and this Movement will spread and blossom until it rapidly encompasses the entire world. Many tribulations and obstacles shall come, but God will remove them all and will fulfil His promise. God addressed me and said: 'I shall grant thee blessing upon blessing until kings shall seek blessings from thy garments!'[20]

So O ye who listen! remember these things and

---

[20] In a vision, I was shown those kings, and they were on horseback. I was told that these are the kings who shall bear the yoke of thy obedience and God shall bless them. [Author]

keep these prophecies safe in your boxes, for they are the words of God that will one day come to pass. I do not observe any goodness in my own self, and I have not done the things which I should have done. I consider myself no more than an unworthy labourer. God's grace was all that helped me through. Therefore, boundless gratitude is due to the All-Powerful and Merciful God Who accepted this handful of dust despite all its ineptitude.

عجب دارم از لطفت اے کردگار
پذیرفتۂ چوں منِ خاکسار
پسندیدگانے بجائے رسند
زما کھترانت چہ آمد پسند
چو از قطرۂ خلق پیدا کنی
همیں عادت اینجا هویدا کنی [21]

I forgot to mention that, in the above-mentioned revelation, the words:

اِنَّ وَعْدَ اللّٰهِ لَا يُبَدَّلُ

---

[21] I marvel at Your benign and marvellous favours upon me
Such that I was granted Your acceptance despite my humility and meekness
With such an abundance of chosen servants under Your majesty
What trait of this humble servant attracted Your fancy?
Just as You created a universe from a droplet
You demonstrated that same attribute here. [Translator]

which mean that God's promise must come to pass, point to the fact that the coming of the five earthquakes is a promise that has to be fulfilled ultimately. Of course, God will have mercy on him who repents and makes peace with Him now, and rids himself of every element of arrogance, but this does not mean that the five promised earthquakes will not come. They will most certainly come, but such people will be saved from the suffering of these quakes, for this is the promise of God, and He never defaults on His promises. Prophecies which contain warning may be averted, but His promises are never averted, as I have earlier stated.

Another question which naturally arises here is that when hundreds of signs had been clearly fulfilled in my support and they were reaching thousands, what was the need for yet another sign of the deadly plague and the devastating earthquakes? Were those hundreds of signs not enough?

This question can be answered in two ways. First, it is the nature of man that he derives very little benefit from signs of God's mercy and compassion. Prejudice causes him to find lame excuses to reject other smaller signs as well and to remain bereft of the fortune of faith. This is what happened here: despite the fulfilment of thousands of signs in my favour, people's hearts were not moved in the least. If you read my book *Nuzūl-ul-Masīḥ,* you shall see for yourselves that there was no scarcity of signs from God in my support. There were signs which were manifested for the benefit of friends, and those which served as warning to the foes. There were signs relating to my person, and signs relating to my children. Just as the oceans cover the greater portion of the earth, so was my Movement filled with heavenly signs. Not a single day goes by without the appearance of a sign. And every prophecy is in itself a sign. In this booklet I have mentioned ten thousand signs just to serve as an illustration. Otherwise, if they were all put into writing, they would make a book of more than a thousand volumes.

Is it possible for a liar to reveal the unseen so abundantly and with such consistency? Each day God continues to bring ignominy upon my ignorant opponents by manifesting all kinds of signs. I swear by Him that just as He granted His converse to the Prophet Abraham[as] and then to Isaac[as], Ishmael[as], Jacob[as], Joseph[as], Moses[as] and Jesus Son of Mary[as], and, after them all, spoke with unmatched clarity and purity to our Prophet Muhammad[sa], so did He honour me with His converse and revelation. But this honour was bestowed upon me solely because of my complete submission to the Holy Prophet Muhammad^{sa}. If I had not been part of the Holy Prophet's^{sa} Ummah, and had not been his follower, then, even if my good deeds had matched all the mountains of the world, I would never have received this honour of converse with God, for all Prophethood has come to an end except the Prophethood of Muhammad^{sa}. No law-bearing Prophet can come after him. A Prophet who does not bring a new law can come, but he has to be a follower of the Holy Prophet^{sa} first. On this basis, I am both an *Ummatī*[22] and a Prophet. My Prophethood, i.e., my converse with God, is nothing but a reflection of the Prophethood of Muhammad^{sa}. Apart from this my Prophethood is nothing. It is the same Prophethood of Muhammad^{sa} which has manifested itself through me. And, since I am a mere reflection of him as well as his devout follower, this does not in the least diminish the high status of the Holy Prophet^{sa}.

The Divine converse which I experience is unequivocal. If I were to doubt it even for an instant, I would become a disbeliever and my afterlife would be ruined. The Word that is revealed to me is certain

---

[22] A follower of the Holy Prophet^{sa}. [Translator]

and definite. Just as no one can doubt the sun and its light when he has seen it, in the same manner, I cannot doubt the veracity of the Word which is revealed to me from God. I believe in it just as I believe in the Book of God. It is possible that, for a time, I might misunderstand the meaning of a particular revelation, but it is impossible for me to have any doubt about it being the Word of God.

By my definition, a Prophet is one upon whom the certain and unequivocal Word of God descends in abundance, and it is such as contains matters of the unseen. It is in this context that God has called me a Prophet, albeit one who does not bring any new law. Till the Day of Judgement, the Holy Quran shall remain the Law-bearing Book.

The word of God which is bestowed upon me has an extraordinary effect and it reveals itself to me with luminous rays. It penetrates my heart like a metal nail and saturates me with its spiritual powers. It is pleasing, eloquent and soothing and is accompanied by Divine awe. It is not niggardly in relating the unseen, and rivers of the unseen flow in it.

As for some of my adversaries who claim to be recipients of Divine Revelation, their revelations do not contain the waves of the unseen, nor do they contain a surging stream of the mysteries of the Divine. Divine Might and Grandeur have, in fact, been nowhere near them. What is more, they themselves confess that they are not sure if their revelations originate from God or from Satan. That is why they usually hold the belief that their revelations have an element of conjecture, for they cannot say if these are from God or Satan.

It is a shame to take pride in such revelations as do not possess enough light even to show that they are truly Divine and have not been inspired by Satan. God is Holy, while Satan is unclean. Hence, strange are these revelations for one cannot even determine with certainty if they originate from a pure fountain or from an impure and polluted one? The other dilemma is that anyone innocently following a satanic revelation, imagining it to be from God, would also fall into the pit of destruction. And conversely, one who does not follow a revelation from God, fearing lest it be from Satan, would also be ruined. So what are these revelations but a frightening dilemma resulting in destruction?

Furthermore, such revelations are a stain on Islam, for the People of Israel were given such unequivocal revelations that the mother of Moses[as] had no doubts about the truth and certainty of the revelation she received and cast her innocent child into the river. The Prophet Khiḍar even killed a child as a result of revelation. But this Ummah (may Allah have mercy on it) did not even attain the spiritual stature that was granted to Israelite women. If this is true, then what is the meaning of the Quranic verse:

$$\text{صِرَاطَ الَّذِيْنَ اَنْعَمْتَ عَلَيْهِمْ}^{23}$$

So are these doubtful revelations of yours—which can equally be ascribed to Raḥmān or to Satan—the blessings (which this verse speaks of)? What a disgrace!

The second answer to the aforementioned question is that, while the prophecies predicting the outcome of even minor incidents are sufficient, as an argument, to establish the truth of God's Messengers—because the sheer number of these prophecies and because the circumstances under which they are made are such that others cannot produce their like—those who are afflicted with scepticism and suspicions continue to be captivated by one doubt or another. For example, if a son is born in a house by the prayers of one who has been

---

[23] The path of those on whom You has bestowed Your blessings. (The Holy Quran, Al-Fātiḥah 1:7) [Publisher]

ordained by Allah, or he gives the glad tiding of a son and a son is born, many would claim that this is not a significant sign. They would say that many women have dreams about themselves, or about women in their neighbourhood, that they have given birth to a son. Now if a son is actually born, in accordance with those dreams, shall we consider such a woman to be Prophet or Messenger or *Muḥaddath**?

These people are not justified in their suspicions, but how can one hold the tongue of the ignorant? They are wrong, because we do not say that the truth of one or two predictions or the accuracy of a few odd dreams are enough to prove that a person is a Messenger and should be considered an elect of God. For that, there should first be a claim, and then there should be prophecies in such numbers and of such quality that the dreams and predictions of ordinary people stand nowhere in comparison to them. As in my case, the number of prophecies regarding the outcome of common incidents that were fulfilled by God at my hand runs into thousands. Who can compete with me in the quantity and quality of the fulfilment of such prophecies?

Some years ago, an unfortunate and ignorant

---

* The one to whom God speaks. [Publisher]

person raised the objection that Maulawī Hakim Nūr-ud-Dīn Sahib lost his son while he is one of my most devoted companions. Although this objection was made out of sheer prejudice and ignorance, considering that our master the Holy Prophet Muhammad[sa] lost eleven of his sons, yet, as a result of my supplications, God revealed to me that Maulawī Hakim Nūr-ud-Dīn Sahib would be granted another son and that this son would later develop boils all over his body as a proof that he is indeed the one who was born as a result of my prayers. This is exactly what happened. A short while after this prophecy, a son was born to Maulawī Sahib and was given the name 'Abdul Ḥa'ī. Shortly after his birth, he developed many boils over his body, the marks of which can still be seen on him. God created those boils on his body so that nobody would think that the birth of the son was the result of a coincidence and not the result of prayers, or that this was not a conclusive proof of the fulfilment of my prophecy.

Sometimes, it so happens that people talk about someone and wish that he were also present. But no sooner have they mentioned his name, than the very person walks in. And the people exclaim: Welcome, it was you we were just talking about.' So God included in my prophecy the sign of the boils on the child's body in order to confirm that the son was born as a result of prayers and not as a mere coincidence. I have thousands of similar illustrations but, unfortunately, it is not possible to catalogue them in this brief booklet.

As I have already mentioned, when prophecies regarding even common incidents number in the thousands, they stand as proof that the person who made the prophecies and who claims to have been sent by Allah is indeed commissioned by Him. Still, those whose hearts suffer from suspicion and scepticism do not desist from casting doubts. They assert that such and such a mendicant had shown a similar miracle, and such and such an astrologer had also said something similar which was later fulfilled. Not only do such people themselves go astray, but they also cause many others to be misled. These unenlightened people possess eyes, but they cannot see all the aspects; they possess a heart, but that heart cannot contemplate on each minute aspect.

When did I ever say that there is no one apart from me who can even have a dream or a revelation? On the contrary, even a prostitute, whose entire life is spent in fornication, can sometimes have true dreams. Even a thief, whose only profession is to steal other people's property, can also be informed of a future incident through a dream.

My claim, which I have repeatedly put before people, is that none but those who have been specially selected by God's grace, are granted dreams and revelations of such substance and quality as number in their thousands, and in respect of which no one else is able to compete with them.

Receiving of true dreams and revelations by ordinary people once in a while is also for the good of mankind. If such a door were entirely shut to the rest of mankind, it would be very difficult for them to believe in the truthfulness of God's Messengers. They would never be able to understand if these Prophets have truly been gifted with Divine Revelation, or if it is a fraud and only the result of some evil temptation. It is in the nature of man that if he has not experienced a phenomenon, he cannot fully comprehend it, and eventually ends up in a state of distrust.

That is why the wine-drinking nations of Europe and America, whose intellects have been blunted by intoxicants, deny the very existence of true dreams, since they do not have any similar experience. Thus, the reason for granting ordinary people an occasional taste of true dreams and revelations is that when a

Prophet appears among them they should not be deprived of the blessing of accepting him. They would know for certain that the phenomenon of revelation is a reality which they have also enjoyed to a limited degree. The difference is that such ordinary people are like beggars who have just a few coins to themselves.............*

---

* For explanation about the incomplete text, please see note on following page which accompanied the third edition of *Tajallīyāt-e-Ilāhiyyah* (Urdu) published in 1950. [Publisher]

An Important Note

This book, entitled *Tajallīyāt-e-Ilāhiyyah,* was printed during the life of the Promised Messiah[as] at Ḍia-ul-Islām Press, under the management of Hakim Faḍluddīn Sahib Bhairwī[ra]. But as the Promised Messiah had not completed writing the book, it was not published at the time.

It was only in 1922 that, with the permission of Ḥaḍrat Khalīfatul Masīḥ II, the book was first published with the addition of the title page. The second edition was published in 1936 and this is the third edition.

The principle we adopt with regard to the writings and books of the Promised Messiah[as] is that we publish them exactly as they were published in the lifetime of the Promised Messiah[as] and under his own supervision. We do not consider it proper to change any of the words on the basis of our own suppositions. In fact, we have not changed even the most evident misprints in this book and have published them exactly as printed in the original.

Jalāl-ud-Dīn Shams
Nāẓir Ta'līf-o-Taṣnīf,
Rabwah, Pakistan.
24th November 1950